Benchmark ADVANCE

Grammar, Spelling & Vocabulary

Activity Book

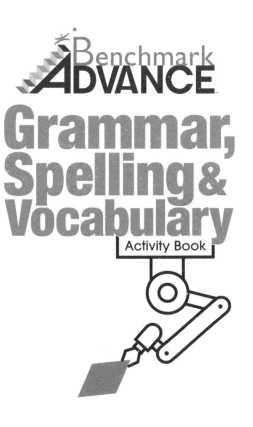

Benchmark Education Company
145 Huguenot Street • New Rochelle, NY 10801

Project Editors: Lisa Yelsey and Rose Birnbaum   Creative Director: Laurie Berger   Art Director: Glenn Davis

Printed in Mexico

ISBN: 978-1-5125-7837-9

Table of Contents

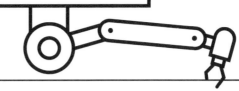

Grammar

Capitalization

Quotation marks are used to set off a speaker's exact words. The first word within the quotation marks is capitalized.

"**L**et's meet on the practice field," said Coach Smith.

Rewrite the sentences using correct capitalization.

1. Mrs. Rodriguez said, "your field trip permission slips are due tomorrow."

_____

2. "do you know what time it is?" asked Mom.

_____

3. "we plan to visit Tucson," I said. "my aunt lives there."

_____

4. The tour guide called out, "everyone should meet at the bus at noon."

_____

5. "when is a snowstorm considered a blizzard?" Mya asked.

_____

6. "see the ducklings?" asked the farmer. "eight eggs hatched last night."

_____

Capitalization

Capitalize the first word in a direct quote.

"**S**ummer is my favorite season," I said. "**W**ho doesn't like summer vacation?"

If the sentence is written correctly, write ✓ on the line. If it is not, write an X on the line and circle any word that should be capitalized.

1. ____ Tina squealed, "our team just won the championship!"

2. ____ "Did you find your backpack?" James asked.

3. ____ "which movie should we see?" I asked.

4. ____ "rainy days are dull," he grumbled. "why isn't the

sun shining?"

5. ____ "Our new puppy is cute," Kym said. "Do you want to

see pictures?"

Rewrite each sentence with correct capitalization.

6. "how much money did we make?" I asked. "should we count again?"

_____

7. Malik asked, "where is the soccer field?"

_____

Punctuate Quotations

A quotation consists of the exact words spoken by a real person or a fictional character. Place the speaker's words in quotation marks. Place a comma after the speaker's introduction or tag, which could end in words such as **said, says**, **states**, **explains**, or **claimed**. Capitalize the first word in the quotation marks.

I read that Benjamin Franklin **said, "H**onesty is the best policy."

My coach always **states, "A**ll I ask is that you do your best."

Each sentence below includes a quotation. Rewrite each sentence using proper punctuation and capitalization.

1. Mark Twain once said when in doubt, tell the truth.

_____

2. I can still hear my piano teacher say first of all, sit up straight!

_____

3. President Truman said if you can't stand the heat, get out of the kitchen.

_____

_____

4. As Mom claims organization is the first step to becoming a genius.

_____

5. I love it when the umpire shouts let's play ball!

_____

6. Shakespeare once wrote there is no darkness but ignorance.

_____

 Grammar, Spelling & Vocabulary Activity Book • © Benchmark Education Company, LLC

Capitalize Proper Nouns

A common noun names a general person, place, or thing.

A proper noun names a specific person, place, or thing.

Each main word in a proper noun should begin with a capital letter.

Common Nouns	Proper Nouns
boy	Seth Collins
school	Parkside Elementary
river	Ohio River

Use the box below to sort and match each common and proper noun. Write each common noun and proper noun with the correct capitalization in the chart.

mountain	april	george washington	city
labor day	mount everest	ocean	president
pacific ocean	holiday	month	chicago

Common Nouns	Proper Nouns

Name _____ Date _____

Combine Sentences

A simple sentence expresses a complete thought. It contains one subject and one predicate. Two simple sentences may be combined to form a compound sentence. Use a comma and a conjunction such as **and**, **or**, **but**, or **so** to join the sentences.

Simple Sentences: The ball hit the window. The glass shattered.

Compound Sentence: The ball hit the window, **and** the glass shattered.

Circle the conjunction that best works to combine the two simple sentences. Then write the compound sentence on the line. Be sure to use a comma.

1. I liked the book.   I didn't like the movie.

   but   so

_____

2. I wanted a new bike.   I started to save my money.

   or   so

_____

3. Sheera went hiking.   Alisa went with her.

   and   or

_____

4. You can buy one large apple.   You can buy two smaller apples.

   but   or

_____

5. It's really hot today.   Let's go to the pool.

   and   so

_____

Punctuate Dialogue

When writing dialogue, place the speaker's words in quotation marks. Place a comma after the speaker's introduction or tag. If the dialogue requires an exclamation point or a question mark, place the punctuation inside the final quotation marks. Place a comma inside the final quotation mark when the speaker's tag follows the speaker's words (do not add a comma if the dialogue ends in a question mark or exclamation point). The first word within the quotation marks should begin with a capital letter.

> "I left my backpack on the bus," Tom said.
>
> He added, "I'm so upset!"
>
> "Did anyone see it?" Tom asked.

Rewrite each sentence adding quotation marks and any other necessary punctuation marks.

1. My friend said You can ride home with us

_____

2. Liza asked When is the next train

_____

3. May I speak with Ms. Kris the caller asked

_____

4. I plan to rake the leaves today said Dad

_____

5. That roller-coaster ride was awesome Maria cried

_____

6. The bank clerk asked How may I help you today

Name _____ Date _____

Informal Language

Informal language has a casual or familiar tone. It is used in personal writing such as friendly letters, texts, and e-mails. Formal language is more precise and careful. It is used in academic writing such as essays. Writers use both informal and formal language in dialogue to show how their characters speak.

Informal: Hey, want to grab lunch?

Formal: I wish to extend an invitation for lunch at noon.

Informal: Lou shouted, "Dude! It's been like forever since I saw you last!"

Formal: Lou said, "Hello, I have not seen you in a long time."

Circle whether each sentence is formal or informal.

1. Let's stop by the skate park after school!

formal   informal

2. I wish to file a complaint about the noise in our neighborhood.

formal   informal

3. Kara rolled her eyes at me, and I totally cracked up!

formal   informal

4. The kid in the last row was like, "Who, me?"

formal   informal

5. I would be grateful if you could send me details about your summer camp.

formal   informal

6. There is no way I'd ever see that scary movie.

formal   informal

Grammar, Spelling & Vocabulary Activity Book • © Benchmark Education Company, LLC   G4 U2 W1 BLM1

Punctuate Dialogue

In dialogue, quotation marks set off a speaker's exact words.

If the speaker is identified before the dialogue, place a comma after the speaker's verb of speech (for example, **said**). Place periods inside quotation marks.

> **The tour guide said,** "Welcome to the museum**.**"

If the speaker is identified after the dialogue, place a comma inside the final quotation mark.

> "I think you will enjoy the exhibits**,"** **he said.**

If the dialogue itself includes a question mark or an exclamation point, place it inside the final quotation mark and drop the comma.

> "Have you seen the new exhibit**?"** **he asked Mariah.**

Circle the sentence that has incorrect punctuation.
Rewrite the sentence, punctuating the dialogue correctly.

1. "Can I borrow a pen?" asked Lily. Anton replied, "You can have this one".

   _____

2. Mom asked, "What time is it?" "It's after four", I told her.

   _____

3. "We won"! Sayeed shouted. "I knew we could do it!" I said.

   _____

4. Mr. Pool said, "Let's go to the store now." "I'd rather go later", Mrs. Pool said.

   _____

5. "Are you ready yet"? Lee asked. "I need five more minutes," Jayden said.

   _____

Complete Sentences

A complete sentence contains a subject and a verb and expresses a complete thought. A sentence fragment is missing a subject or a verb or both, so it does not express a complete thought.

Fragment: Set behind the hills.

Complete Sentence: The evening sun set behind the hills.

Circle the word or phrase that is missing from the sentence fragment. Then rewrite each complete sentence correctly.

1. The Colorado River.

runs through the Grand Canyon   a national park

_____

2. Are nocturnal, which means they are active at night.

all bats   sleeps during the day

_____

3. The Australian koala.

is a fussy eater   kangaroos and wombats

_____

4. Earth's tides.

a lunar eclipse   are caused by the moon

_____

5. Different kinds of animals.

live in the Arctic   many natural resources

_____

Name _____ Date _____

Correct Spelling

If you are unsure of how to spell a certain word, you should look it up in a dictionary. Words in a dictionary are listed alphabetically. A print dictionary includes two guide words at the top of each page, which help you figure out if the word you are looking up is on the page. All words that come between the two guide words can be found on the page.

Guide words: shellfish • **sho**ck

Included on the page: shiver

Not included: shutter

Circle the correct pair of guide words for each word.

1. demolish

delicious • dense   deny • desert

2. enlarge

endure • engine   enemy • enormous

3. florist

fleet • flurry   fluster • foliage

4. jaunty

jagged • jawbone   jay • jester

5. meddle

mean • measles   mechanic • mellow

6. pledge

plot • plum   planet • pliers

7. animal

apple • atlas   album • annual

Interrogative Pronouns

An interrogative pronoun is used to introduce a question. The pronoun represents the person or object that is the subject of the question. **Who**, **what**, **which**, and **whose** are interrogative pronouns. **Who** is used to ask questions about people. **What** and **which** are used to ask questions about animals or things. **Whose** is used to ask questions about possession.

Who wants to go to the park?

What is your pet's name?

Which of the snakes is poisonous?

Whose book is this?

Circle the correct interrogative pronoun to complete each question.

1. of the eastern states grows the most strawberries?

Who   What   Which   Whose

2. needs a ride to the game?

Who   What   Which   Whose

3. is our homework for tomorrow?

Who   What   Which   Whose

4. uniform was left in the locker room?

Who   What   Which   Whose

5. is the new teacher's name?

Who   What   Which   Whose

6. birthday is in April?

Who   What   Which   Whose

Grammar, Spelling & Vocabulary Activity Book • © Benchmark Education Company, LLC

Frequently Misspelled Words

One strategy to help you spell correctly is to sound out the word and match the sounds to the letters. Another is to look up the word in a dictionary. The words listed below are often misspelled.

always	believe	friend	grateful	independence
knowledge	necessary	occurred	perceive	recommend
scissors	similar	Tuesday	vacuum	weird

Circle the misspelled word in each sentence. Rewrite the word on the line with the correct spelling.

1. Learning to build a fire is a nesessary skill for camping.

_____

2. Which movie do you reccommend that we see on Tuesday?

_____

3. Our team uniform is similiar to that of the Jaguars. _____

4. I can't beleive how much snow fell today! _____

5. Mom always reminds me that knowlege is power. _____

6. I was greatful for all the help from my teammates. _____

7. I don't like movies with wierd characters. _____

8. A friend told us what occured at the chess club meeting.

_____

Capitalization

Always capitalize the first and last words in a title as well as the main words of the title: nouns, pronouns, verbs, adjectives, and adverbs.
Do not capitalize articles **a**, **an**, and **the**, and most short prepositions, such as **at**, **in**, **by**, **for**, **of**, and **to**.

I just read <u>**T**he **S**ong of the **W**hales</u>.

<u>**I**n a **S**ea of **F**ury</u> is one of my favorite books.

Circle the words in the underlined book titles that should be capitalized.

1. My book report is on <u>a house by the sea</u>.

2. I borrowed <u>the spiders of north america</u> from the library.

3. Have you seen my book, <u>in the caves</u>?

4. The author of <u>survival in antarctica</u> visited our school.

5. I bought <u>hiking tips for beginners</u> to take on our trip.

Rewrite each sentence using correct capitalization for the underlined book title.

6. I just finished reading the <u>best way to train a dog</u>.

_____

7. I read a book called <u>food and science</u> to learn about cooking.

_____

Punctuate Dialogue

When writing dialogue, quotation marks are used to set off the speaker's exact words. Capitalize the first word in the quotation marks. If the speaker is identified before the dialogue, a comma is placed after the speaker's tag, before the first quotation mark. If the speaker is identified after the dialogue, the comma goes inside the final quotation mark. When an exclamation point or question mark is part of the dialogue itself, place the punctuation inside the quotation mark and drop the final comma. A period always goes inside the quotation marks.

> I asked, "Who has a flashlight?"
>
> "I have one," Marta answered.
>
> "Me, too!" called Paolo.

Rewrite each sentence using correct punctuation.

1. Is this your usual bus stop I asked

_____

2. Cecily shouted Our team just won first place

_____

3. Today will be sunny and mild said the weather forecaster

_____

4. Jamal asked Is everyone ready to go.

_____

5. Will you set the table, please asked Mom

_____

6. The tour guide said This painting has an interesting history

_____

7. I asked can we go for a hike tomorrow

_____

Complete Sentences

A complete sentence contains a subject and a verb, and expresses a complete thought. A sentence fragment is missing a subject or a verb or both, so it does not express a complete thought.

Fragment Missing a Subject: Ran away from the dog.

Corrected: The boy ran away from the dog.

Fragment Missing a Verb: The colorful bird a nest.

Corrected: The colorful bird **built** a nest.

Circle whether each fragment is missing a subject or a verb. Then choose a phrase from the box to complete each sentence. Rewrite the fragment as a complete sentence.

crunched under our feet	hibernate in winter	my little sister
a NASA astronaut	an old steam train	has a deadly bite

1. Chugged into the depot.

subject   verb

_____

2. A coral snake.

subject   verb

_____

3. The dried fallen leaves.

subject   verb

_____

4. Wrote a book about going into space.

subject   verb

_____

   Grammar, Spelling & Vocabulary Activity Book • © Benchmark Education Company, LLC

Combine Sentences

One way to combine sentences is by using **and** or **or** to join two subjects (but only if the same predicate appears in both sentences) or join two predicates (if the same subject appears in both sentences).

Lisa ran a marathon. **Althea** ran a marathon.

Lisa and Althea ran a marathon.

The child **cried.** The child **threw her toy**.

The child **cried and threw her toy**.

Rewrite each pair of sentences, combining the two sentences to form one sentence.

1. The storm hit Springfield. The storm destroyed the town.

_____

2. The Jaguars made it to the semifinals. The Dragons made it to the semifinals.

_____

3. I walk to school every other day. I bike to school every other day.

_____

4. Oranges contain vitamin C. Strawberries contain vitamin C.

_____

5. The kite snapped the string. The kite got caught in a tree.

_____

6. My mom told funny family stories. Mom's cousins told funny family stories.

_____

7. According to the forecast, it may rain tonight. It may snow tonight.

_____

Name _____ Date _____

Capitalize Proper Nouns

Always capitalize a proper noun. If a proper noun contains more than one word, capitalize the first and last words, as well as any other main words like nouns, pronouns, verbs, adjectives, and adverbs.

On **Monday, Marcus** visited the **Statue** of **Liberty**.

In **May,** the **Smith** family will go to the **Museum** of **Natural History**.

Circle the first letter of the proper nouns that should be capitalized. Then rewrite the sentence correctly.

1. Our neighbor, mr. allen, works at a restaurant called noodles and tea.

_____

2. Is parkland mall on the corner of market street and jerome avenue?

_____

3. Aunt nora and uncle jeff met in new york.

_____

4. Have you visited the amherst sports and fitness center yet?

_____

5. My teacher asked dr. ingram to tell us about the international space station.

_____

6. Mom and dad both work at the kenlake building on seahawk avenue.

_____

 G4 U3 W3 BLM1

Interrogative Pronouns

An interrogative pronoun is a word used to introduce a question. **Who, whom,** and **whose** refer to people. **What** and **which** refer to animals and things. **Who, what,** and **which** are subject pronouns. **Whom** is an object pronoun. **Whose** shows possession.

    Who lost a backpack?   To **whom** did you speak?

    What breed is that dog?   **What** is the capital of Maine?

    Which cat is the friendliest?   **Whose** hat is this?

Write an interrogative pronoun to complete each question.

1. _____ wants to go to the concert with me?

2. _____ one of the bikes is yours?

3. _____ do you plan to prepare for dinner?

4. To _____ was the angry letter sent?

5. _____ book report was turned in without a name on it?

6. _____ was the final score of the game?

7. _____ of the teams has the most home runs?

8. _____ sneakers are these?

9. To _____ did the league award the trophy?

10. _____ wants to go ice-skating on Saturday?

Name _____ Date _____

Relative Adverbs

The words **when**, **where**, and **why** may be used as relative adverbs. A relative adverb introduces a relative clause and refers to a time, a place, or a reason. The relative clause gives more information about a word or phrase in the sentence.

> **A Time:** April is usually the month **when** the cherry trees bloom.
> **A Place:** Texas is **where** my cousins live.
> **A Reason:** I know the reason **why** our field trip was canceled.

Underline the relative clause. Then, circle the relative adverb.

1. Monday is when I have my piano lesson.

2. France is where my pen pal lives.

3. I'll always remember the day when I hit my first home run.

4. Our principal explained the reason why the buses would be late.

5. I visited Holland, where I always wanted to go.

6. It was 1939 when my grandparents came to America.

7. The scientist explained the phenomenon behind why the sun is boiling hot.

8. My mom drove me to the town where my friend lives.

Grammar, Spelling & Vocabulary Activity Book • © Benchmark Education Company, LLC

Punctuate Dialogue

If the speaker is identified first, place a comma after the speaker's tag, before the first quotation mark. If the speaker is identified after the dialogue, place a comma inside the final quotation mark (do not add a comma if the dialogue ends in a question mark or exclamation point). Note that a question mark or an exclamation point goes inside the final quotation mark only if it is part of the dialogue.

Sayeed asked**,** "Who wants to go to the park tomorrow**?"**

"I'm free tomorrow**,"** Marco said.

"Me, too**!"** said Marco's sister.

Write _C_ if the sentence is punctuated correctly. Write _X_ if it is not, and then rewrite the sentence using correct punctuation and capitalization.

1. _____ Which bus stops at Market Street? Mom asked.

_____

2. _____ Dad answered, "I think the Blue Line goes to Market Street."

_____

3. _____ I'm pretty sure the Blue Line ends before Market Street, I said.

_____

4. _____ Mom asked are you sure?

_____

5. _____"I think so, but let's check the map," I said.

_____

6. _____ Dad agreed and said, that would make sense.

_____

Progressive Verb Tenses

Progressive verb tenses show ongoing or continuous action. A progressive verb tense is formed by using a **to be** verb and the **-ing** form of an action verb.

Present Progressive: I **am walking** to school by myself this morning.
Past Progressive: My sister and I **were walking** together yesterday.
Future Progressive: We **will be walking** together tomorrow, too.

For each sentence, circle the verb tense of the underlined words.

1. Nica and I <u>are studying</u> together.

present progressive   past progressive   future progressive

2. Our neighbor <u>will be moving</u> next week.

present progressive   past progressive   future progressive

3. I <u>was having</u> dinner when the doorbell rang.

present progressive   past progressive   future progressive

Complete each sentence. Use the verb tense and verb named in ( ) to fill in the blank.

4. My sister _____ to Denmark next year.
(future progressive of **travel**)

5. When I last saw the campers, they _____ a fire.
(past progressive of **build**)

6. Mom _____ Spanish at the high school today.
(present progressive of **teach**)

Grammar, Spelling & Vocabulary Activity Book • © Benchmark Education Company, LLC   G4 U4 W2 BLM1

Frequently Confused Words

Homophones are words that sound the same but have different spellings and meanings. Some homophones are **to/two/too**, **board/bored**, **sun/son**, **hear/here**, **there/their/they're**, **it's/its**. Think about all the possible meanings of a homophone, and use the word with the meaning intended in the sentence.

I went **to** the store and the post office, **too**. I mailed **two** letters. The turtles laid **their** eggs over **there** in the sand. **They're** buried safely near the rocks.

Circle the correct word or words to complete each sentence.

1. Tell the twins to put (their, there, they're) toys in the box
over (their, there, they're).

2. Let's go (to, too, two) the library after lunch and stay until
(to, too, two) o'clock.

3. Simon thinks that the spelling words are (to, too, two) difficult.

4. Look over (their, there, they're), and you will see (to, too, two)
elephants.

5. The puppies are cute, and (their, there, they're)
friendly, (to, too, two).

6. (Its, It's) so noisy in (hear, here).

7. If you come (right, write) now, you can have a (peace, piece)
of pie.

8. I want to sit over (there, their, they're) so that I can (hear, here)
the speaker when he comes on the stage.

Relative Pronouns

The words **who**, **whom**, **whose**, **that**, and **which** may be used as relative pronouns. A relative pronoun introduces a relative clause that tells more about a word in the sentence.

The relative clause . . .	**Tells more about . . .**
I know a man **who** works for NASA.	man
Here is my aunt for **whom** we were waiting.	aunt
The students **whose** work is done may go out.	students
The shoes **that** Mom bought were too small.	shoes
The birds, **which** nest in our trees, are red.	birds

Circle the correct relative pronoun in ( ) to complete each sentence. Underline the word that the relative clause tells more about.

1. Lin helped the woman (who/which) dropped her grocery bag.

2. The boxes (that/who) the movers needed were left at the curb.

3. The people (which/whose) homes were damaged went to the shelter.

4. This bike, (who/which) is my favorite color, is too expensive.

5. My friend for (who/whom) the party was given was very surprised.

6. The man (whom/who) is waiting for the bus is my dad.

7. The jacket (that/who) I picked out is very warm.

8. Max helped the neighbors (when/whose) dog ran away.

Punctuate Quotations

If the person being quoted is identified first, place a comma before the first quotation mark. Place the quote's end punctuation inside the final quotation mark. If the person being quoted is identified after the quotation, place a comma inside the final quotation mark. A question mark or an exclamation point that is part of the quotation goes inside the quotation mark, but do not add a comma after the question mark or exclamation point.

The author states, "Ants have been on Earth for millions of years."

"Human exploration of Mars will happen soon," Allen says.

"The life cycle of a frog is amazing!" said the scientist.

Rewrite each sentence with the correct punctuation for the quotation.

1. President Lincoln once said, Whatever you are, be a good one.

_____

2. We are working to bring the seals back to the island, Dr. Kellman reported.

_____

_____

3. The mayor announced, We plan to build a soccer field with the excess funds.

_____

_____

4. Marie Curie made the statement, Be less curious about people and more curious about ideas.

_____

_____

 Grammar, Spelling & Vocabulary Activity Book • © Benchmark Education Company, LLC

Adjective Order

Follow this order when using more than one adjective to describe a noun: opinion (**nice, angry, delicious**), size (**large, long**), look/feel (**broken, soft**), age (**new, old**), color (**red, purple**), origin (**American, Mexican**), material (**wooden, gold**).

We have an **energetic, young** dog with **long, brown** ears. He loves to sleep on our **big, soft, red** couch.

Complete the following sentences by writing the adjectives in ( ) in the correct order.

1. The _____, _____, _____ bunny wiggled its nose at me.

(soft   brown   cute)

2. Did you see the _____, _____ hot-air balloon over the

stadium?   (colorful   huge)

3. I ordered a _____, _____, _____ salad.

(big   Greek   delicious)

4. Tim got a _____, _____, _____ bike for his birthday.

(red   beautiful   shiny)

5. A _____, _____ snake slithered out of the bushes.

(striped   long)

6. Did anyone find a _____, _____, _____ backpack?

(purple   large   new)

Compound Sentences with Coordinating Conjunctions

A coordinating conjunction can be used to join two simple sentences to form a compound sentence. The words **and** and **but** are coordinating conjunctions. **And** connects similar ideas. **But** shows a contrast. A comma before the coordinating conjunction shows where one sentence ends and the other starts.

I returned a library book**, and** I checked out an audiobook.

I practice the piano every day**, but** I don't seem to improve.

Rewrite the two simple sentences to make a compound sentence. Use *and* or *but* and a comma.

1. I rushed to the ticket office. The concert was sold out.

_____

2. I studied for my math test. I got a good grade.

_____

3. The kale was on sale. I do not really like kale.

_____

4. We went to the street fair. Mom bought us roasted corn.

_____

5. Dad took me shopping. He realized he'd left his wallet at home.

_____

6. My sister made sandwiches for lunch. I helped clean up afterward.

_____

Modal Auxiliaries

A modal auxiliary is a verb that helps the main verb of a sentence express a particular meaning or idea. The words **may, can, must,** and **should** are modal auxiliaries. **May** expresses permission or a probability. **Can** expresses an ability to do something. **Must** expresses a necessity. **Should** expresses something that is expected.

Jessa **may** visit this weekend. If she comes, we **can** meet her at the bus station. We **should** plan what to do. We **must** take her to see the new baby panda at the zoo.

Circle the modal auxiliary that expresses the correct meaning of each sentence.

1. If I have the time, I (can , must) rake the leaves tomorrow.

2. My parents said I (may, must) call if I'm going to be home late.

3. Even though you don't think it's your fault, you (can, should) apologize and talk through a resolution to the problem.

4. All the votes aren't in yet, but it looks as if Desi (must, may) win the election.

5. Mom said she (can, must) run every day to be ready for the marathon.

6. (May, Should) we leave the house earlier to make sure we're on time?

7. (May , Should) I have another orange?

8. After lots of training, my dog (must, can) do five tricks.

Compound Sentences with Coordinating Conjunctions

A coordinating conjunction connects two simple sentences to form a compound sentence. The words **or** and **so** are coordinating conjunctions. **Or** shows a choice. **So** shows a cause-effect relationship. A comma before the coordinating conjunction shows where one sentence ends and the other starts.

I can have lunch first, **or** I can clean my room now.

It's raining, **so** the game has been called off.

Rewrite the two sentences to make a compound sentence. Use *or* or *so* and a comma.

1. You can visit your grandmother today. You can wait until tomorrow.

_____

2. We ran out of flour. We couldn't make cookies.

_____

3. You can make a poster to advertise the sale. You can create a video ad.

_____

4. We can visit the Natural History Museum. We can spend the day at the Art Museum.

_____

5. I want to help my family. I'll wash the dishes.

_____

6. We can practice today. We can wait to practice tomorrow.

_____

Prepositional Phrases

A prepositional phrase is a group of words that includes a preposition and a noun or pronoun along with any modifiers. Prepositional phrases often answer questions such as **where, when, what for,** or **how.**

Where?	I put the fruit salad **on** the kitchen table.
When?	I have a dentist appointment **after** school.
What for?	I need to buy some clay **for** the art project.
How?	Mom melted the frozen car door **with** a hair dryer.

Circle the word that completes each sentence correctly. Then write it on the line.

1. Dina answered the teacher's question _____ her usual confidence.

    of   with

2. Paul found an old silver coin _____ a pile of rubble.

    after   under

3. I studied the spelling words _____ my lunch break.

    below   during

4. Shanice plans to save her allowance _____ a new tablet.

    with   for

5. I wrote a funny poem _____ a talking cat.

    about   across

6. I asked Mom to order one pizza _____ cheese.

    into   without

7. I practice the piano _____ dinner.

    after   with

Name _____ Date _____

Compound Sentences with Coordinating Conjunctions

A coordinating conjunction joins two sentences to form a compound sentence. **So** and **yet** are coordinating conjunctions. **So** shows a cause-effect relationship. **Yet** shows a contrast. A comma before the coordinating conjunction shows where one sentence ends and the other starts.

I want to help my team**, so** I'll practice my kicking skills.

I have never visited Vermont**, yet** have I been to New Hampshire.

Rewrite the two sentences to make a compound sentence. Use *so* or *yet* and a comma.

1. I didn't finish my math last night. I worked on it this morning.

_____

2. I haven't seen Tia in a while. I know we will have fun together.

_____

3. It rained all day. Dad has to wait to mow the lawn.

_____

4. It may rain later. It's sunny outside now.

_____

5. I want to earn some money this summer. I'm going to walk dogs.

_____

6. Gramps is coming to visit. I'm helping to make his favorite meal.

_____

Name _____ Date _____

Correct Spelling

A print dictionary has two guide words at the top of each page. The guide word on the left represents the first entry on the page, and the one on the right represents the last entry on the page. Only the words that come between the two guide words can be found on the page.

Guide words: gadget • gasp

Included on the page: game

Not included: gather

For each pair of guide words, write *yes* or *no* to answer the question.

1. adapt • advancement

Is the word **address** on this page? _____

2. chairman • chowder

Is the word **chute** on this page? _____

3. falcon • fathom

Is the word **fastener** on this page? _____

4. lagoon • lava

Is the word **laughter** on this page? _____

5. necessary • neighbor

Is the word **nervous** on this page? _____

6. pail • partner

Is the word **panel** on this page? _____

7. dog • domestic

Is the word **donate** on this page? _____

8. service • setter

Is the word **session** on this page? _____

Grammar, Spelling & Vocabulary Activity Book • © Benchmark Education Company, LLC   G4 U6 W1 BLM1

Adjective Order

Follow this order when using more than one adjective to describe a noun: opinion (**happy**, **beautiful**), size (**tiny**, **long**), look/feel (**round**, **shiny**, **rough**), age (**young**, **old**, **antique**), color (**blue**, **clear**), origin (**European**), material (**cotton**, **silver**). Use a comma after each adjective. However, never use a comma between the last adjective and the noun.

> **Incorrect:** Mom gave me a sparkly, fabulous, bracelet.
>
> **Correct:** Mom gave me a **fabulous, sparkly** bracelet.

Rewrite each sentence by adding the adjectives in ( ) to describe the underlined noun. Use the correct adjective order and punctuation.

1. Mara's dog has <u>fur</u>. (brown silky long)

_____

2. The <u>car</u> zipped past the finish line. (red small)

_____

3. My grandparents live in a <u>farmhouse</u>. (old charming yellow)

_____

4. Mom made a <u>pasta salad</u>. (colorful yummy big)

_____

5. I found a <u>camera</u> in the attic. (cracked antique strange)

_____

6. I made a <u>tail</u> for my kite. (shiny long)

_____

Punctuate Dialogue

When writing dialogue, place the speaker's words in quotation marks. Use a comma to separate the speaker's introduction or tag from the speaker's words. Place a comma inside the final quotation mark when the speaker's tag follows the speaker's words. The first word within the quotation marks should begin with a capital letter. However, if the speaker's words are interrupted, do not capitalize the first word in the continued quotation.

Sena asked, "**D**id you finish reading your book?"

"**N**ot yet," Max answered.

"**I**'ve started it," Max said, "**b**ut I'm only halfway through."

"**I**f you like that book," Sena said, "**y**ou'll really like this one."

Rewrite each sentence using correct punctuation and capitalization.

1. Jan asked would you like to come to my party?

_____

2. Turn left on Oak Street Bill explained and then right on Smith.

_____

3. I'm looking for a book in Spanish Mom said to the clerk.

_____

4. For our field trip Mr. Marzo said let's visit the planetarium.

_____

5. Before moving to Chicago I explained we lived in Tucson.

_____

6. I bought Dad a book for his birthday I told Mom.

_____

 Grammar, Spelling & Vocabulary Activity Book • © Benchmark Education Company, LLC

Name _____ Date _____

Frequently Confused Words

Some words sound the same but are spelled differently and have different meanings. These words are called homophones. Some examples of homophones include **break/brake, principal/principle, knight/night,** and **flu/flew.**

Our **principal** makes it a **principle** to listen to both sides of a story.

Circle the two words that sound the same in each sentence. Then write the one word that completes the definition correctly.

1. Which one of the twins won first place?

   Achieved victory is another meaning for _____.

2. I put a bandage over the cut on my heel to help it heal.

   Cure is another word for _____.

3. My dentist treats all her patients with a lot of patience.

   Calmness is another word for _____.

4. The storm damaged the beautiful capitol in the state capital.

   "A building where lawmakers meet" is the definition of

   _____.

5. Did you break both the chain and the brake on your bike?

   A device that helps a wheel stop is a _____.

6. Wow, the historical site was a fantastic sight!

   Location is another word for _____.

7. The tale of the fox with a red tail amused us.

   Story is another word for _____.

Compound Sentences with Coordinating Conjunctions

A compound sentence is made up of two sentences joined by a comma and a coordinating conjunction.

I sent the email, **and** I received a reply immediately.

Jerri ran to the station, **but** she missed the train by minutes.

Laws are important, **for** they help keep us safe.

We can go to the café, **or** we can make lunch here.

It was too hot out, **so** I went inside.

Rewrite each pair of sentences to make a compound sentence. Use a comma and one of the following coordinating conjunctions: *and*, *but*, *for*, *or*, *so*.

1. Mila went to the seashore. She took lots of photographs there.

_____

2. I really didn't have time to play. I didn't want to disappoint my little brother.

_____

3. We're out of cereal. I'll make scrambled eggs instead.

_____

4. This morning is sunny and clear. An afternoon storm has been forecast.

_____

5. I need to finish my homework now. I'll have to do it this weekend.

_____

6. I was tired after the bike ride. It was all uphill.

_____

 Grammar, Spelling & Vocabulary Activity Book • © Benchmark Education Company, LLC

Relative Pronouns

A relative pronoun introduces a relative clause that tells more about a word in the sentence. **Who, whom,** and **whose** refer to people. **That** and **which** refer to things or people.

The relative clause	**Tells more about**
I have a pen pal **who** lives in Denmark.	pen pal
This is my cousin, for **whom** we were waiting.	cousin
The contestant **whose** name I call may come forward.	contestant
The boxes **that** we found will be perfect for moving.	boxes
The pug, **which** is my favorite breed, won the dog show.	pug

Circle the relative pronoun in ( ) that correctly completes each sentence. Then underline the word that the relative clause tells more about.

1. These are the muffins (who, that) Mikos baked.

2. The person (who, which) guesses the correct number will get a prize.

3. The girl (whom, whose) essay won the contest will visit our class.

4. The truck, (whose, which) was hauling peaches, ran into a ditch.

5. The candidate, with (who, whom) I agree, took a firm stand on that issue.

6. The plants (that, who) bloom faster get the most attention.

Punctuation for Effect

Use an exclamation point at the end of a statement that shows strong emotion, such as excitement, surprise, happiness, or fear. Use a period at the end of a statement that does not show strong emotion.

Not strong emotion: I entered a painting in the art contest.

Strong emotion: I couldn't believe that I won first prize!

Circle whether each statement shows strong emotion or not. Then write the appropriate end punctuation on the line.

1. We got so much snow yesterday ____

strong emotion   not strong emotion

2. Marta went to get out the snow shovel ____

strong emotion   not strong emotion

3. Oh no, I lost my wallet ____

strong emotion   not strong emotion

4. I walked around the corner ____

strong emotion   not strong emotion

5. I couldn't believe my eyes ____

strong emotion   not strong emotion

6. Suddenly, a fierce dog came running at me ____

strong emotion   not strong emotion

Prepositional Phrases

A prepositional phrase is a group of words that includes a preposition and a noun or pronoun along with any modifiers.

Prepositional phrases often answer questions such as **where**, **when**, **how**, or **how long**.

The book fell **behind the shelf.**   Fix the torn poster **with tape.**

I called home **during halftime.**   The war lasted **for six years.**

Underline the prepositional phrase in each sentence. Then circle the question that the prepositional phrase answers.

1. Marco studied his history notes before the test.

   When?   Where?   How?   How long?

2. The frightened kitten ran under the porch.

   When?   Where?   How?   How long?

3. I held the tiny kitten with great care.

   When?   Where?   How?   How long?

4. We picked up lots of broken branches after the storm.

   When?   Where?   How?   How long?

5. Sarah hiked for an hour.

   When?   Where?   How?   How long?

6. The extremely tired campers crawled into their tents.

   When?   Where?   How?   How long?

Precise Language

Use precise words and phrases to convey your ideas when you write. Precise language makes your writing clearer and more interesting because the reader is able to visualize what is being described.

Not Precise: The horse **ran** across the field.

Precise: The horse **galloped** across the field.

For each sentence, circle the words in ( ) that are more precise. Then write the complete sentence on the line.

1. Mr. Franklin (walked, trudged) along with the (enormous, big) box.

_____

_____

2. The child (howled, cried) when she dropped her (toy, fuzzy bear).

_____

_____

3. A snake will often (make a sound, hiss) to (warn, tell) others of its presence.

_____

_____

4. The (bad, destructive) tornado (went, ripped) through the town.

_____

_____

5. Butterflies (go, flutter) from plant to plant (looking for, seeking) food.

_____

_____

Complete Sentences

A complete sentence contains a subject and a verb, and expresses a complete thought. A fragment is missing a subject, a verb, or both, and does not express a complete thought.

Sentence Fragment: The rock climber the avalanche.

Complete Sentence: The rock climber survived the avaianche.

Determine whether each sentence is a complete sentence or a fragment. If it is a complete sentence, write *CS* on the line. For a fragment, write what is missing on the line: *subject* or *verb*.

1. The clock in the old bell tower. _____

2. Our team won the championship. _____

3. Snow is predicted for tonight. _____

4. Worried about her spelling test. _____

5. Suddenly, started to rain. _____

Rewrite each pair of sentences, combining the two fragments to make one complete sentence.

6. The first people to explore the river. Discovered a waterfall.

_____

7. Yesterday, my best friend. Sprained his ankle.

_____

 Grammar, Spelling & Vocabulary Activity Book • © Benchmark Education Company, LLC

Frequently Confused Words

Words that sound the same but have different spellings and meanings are frequently confused. To avoid reader confusion, make sure to use the version of the word that expresses the intended meaning as it is used in the sentence.

Did you **hear** the thunderstorm last night?

The speaker should be **here** by noon.

Circle the word that completes each sentence correctly. Then write the word on the line.

1. Please _____ the door before you leave today.

close   clothes

2. What do you plan to _____ with your birthday money?

by   buy   bye

3. I liked the movie, but my mom was completely _____.

board   bored

4. The tourists bought _____ tickets on a travel website.

there   their   they're

5. Have you finished _____ homework yet?

you're   your

6. We drove _____ the tunnel to get to New York City.

threw   through

7. Carla ordered the soup and a sandwich, _____.

to   two   too

8. We'll meet you at the movies in an _____.

hour   our

Grammar, Spelling & Vocabulary Activity Book • © Benchmark Education Company, LLC

Correct Run-Ons

A run-on sentence contains two or more complete sentences that are missing punctuation or a conjunction. One way to correct a run-on sentence is to divide the two complete sentences into two separate sentences.

Run-On Sentence: The bus ran late Jamie missed his first class.

Corrected: The bus ran late. Jamie missed his first class.

Correct each run-on sentence by rewriting it as two separate sentences.

1. The campers found a clearing near the lake they set up their tents.

_____

2. Mom made two cakes for the bake sale I decorated them.

_____

3. We heard the thunder rumble the wind howled through the trees.

_____

4. Mr. Ataro collects antique pens he has over two hundred.

_____

5. The garden club meets monthly the members have planted dozens of trees.

_____

6. Dad teaches art at the community center he has fifteen students.

_____

Name _____ Date _____

Progressive Verb Tenses

Progressive verb tenses show ongoing or continuous action. The progressive form of a main verb is formed by adding **-ing** to the end of the verb. The tense depends on the tense of the **to be** verb that comes before the main verb.

Present Progressive Tense: formed by placing the word **am**, **is**, or **are** in front of the **-ing** form of the verb. Example: Jon **is working** today.

Past Progressive Tense: formed by placing the word **was** or **were** in front of the **-ing** form of the verb. Example: Jon **was working** from 9 to 5 yesterday.

Future Progressive Tense: formed by inserting the words **will be** in front of the **-ing** form of the verb. Example: Jon **will be working** six hours tomorrow.

Write the correct progressive tense of the verb in ( ) to complete each sentence.

1. Mr. Wilson _____ art next year. (teach)

2. Mom _____ over the bridge right now. (drive)

3. When we arrived, our parents _____ at the gate. (wait)

4. Our neighbors _____ on vacation next month. (go)

5. At this moment, Kia and Jack _____ a cartoon. (watch)

6. Today the sun is shining, but yesterday it _____ hard. (rain)

7. I _____ many books next summer break. (read)

Grammar, Spelling & Vocabulary Activity Book • © Benchmark Education Company, LLC G4 U8 W1 BLM1

Punctuate Dialogue

When writing dialogue, quotation marks are used to set off the speaker's exact words. Capitalize the first word in the quotation marks. If the speaker is identified first, a comma is placed after the speaker's tag, before the first quotation mark. If the speaker is identified after the dialogue, the comma goes inside the final quotation mark. When an exclamation point or a question mark is part of the dialogue itself, place the punctuation inside the quotation mark. A period always goes inside the quotation mark.

Tia said**,** "I think I lost my book**.**"

"The title is *Adventures in Time***,**" she added.

"Where did you have it last**?**" I asked.

"Here it is**!**" Danny shouted.

Rewrite each sentence using correct punctuation and capitalization for the dialogue.

1. Who wants to go to the pool today Mom asked.

_____

2. Mr. Sanders cried this hiking trail is 20 miles long!

_____

3. Wow, the turtle eggs hatched last night Mike exclaimed.

_____

4. Mrs. Kiel announced kids now it's time to go to the library.

_____

5. Let's stop for lemonade Dad suggested.

_____

6. Mike asked do you have a pencil that I could borrow?

_____

Interrogative Pronouns and Relative Pronouns

An interrogative pronoun introduces a question. A relative pronoun introduces a clause that gives more information about the subject of a sentence. Some examples of interrogative and relative pronouns include **who**, **whom**, **whose**, **that**, and **which**. The way the pronoun is used in a sentence determines whether it is an interrogative or a relative pronoun.

Interrogative Pronoun: Who is knocking at the door?

Relative Pronoun: The man **who** is knocking at the door is our neighbor.

Circle the pronoun in each sentence. On the line, write *IP* if it is used as an interrogative pronoun or *RP* if it is used as a relative pronoun.

1. _____ Which store has the best selection?

2. _____ The picnic, which was held at the park, was so much fun!

3. _____ Pat got the autograph of the man who climbed Mt. Everest.

4. _____ Who knows how to fix a flat tire?

5. _____ Whose notebook is this?

6. _____ The contestants whose names were chosen gave a big cheer.

Write the pronoun that completes each sentence correctly.

7. _____ time are you going to the movies?

8. The woman _____ drives the school bus is my neighbor.

Correct Run-Ons

A run-on sentence contains two or more complete sentences that are not joined with correct punctuation or a conjunction. One way to correct a run-on sentence is to divide it into two or more separate complete sentences, each with a subject and a verb.

Run-On: It hasn't rained for days many of the plants are dry.

Correction: It hasn't rained for days. Many of the plants are dry.

Rewrite the following run-on sentences as two separate sentences.

1. The seashore is so beautiful at sunset I've taken many photos.

_____

2. Did anyone lose a backpack I found a blue one in the lunchroom.

_____

3. A butterfly landed on the flower it was sipping the nectar.

_____

4. I learned how to snorkel last summer it was so much fun!

_____

5. I can't believe I won first prize this is the most exciting day of my life!

_____

6. Do all bears hibernate I want to find a book on bears of North America.

_____

7. I am going to the library the librarians are teaching a class about doing research.

_____

Order Adjectives

Follow this order when using more than one adjective to describe a noun: number (**two, many**), opinion (**kind, delicious**), size (**short, huge**), look/feel (**cold, silky**), age (**new, old**), shape (**oblong, rectangular**), color (**green, multicolored**), origin (**American, Asian**), material (**paper, wooden**). Place a comma after each adjective, except a number. Never use a comma between the last adjective and the noun.

Incorrect: I have two, fuzzy, amazing, large, dogs.

Correct: I have **two amazing, large, fuzzy** dogs.

For each sentence, read the two choices below the sentence and circle the letter showing the adjectives listed in the correct order. Then rewrite the adjectives on the line using correct punctuation.

1. Mia always takes _____ shopping bags to the market.

  a. two huge green   b. green huge two

2. I'm going to knit a _____ scarf.

  a. soft colorful long   b. long soft colorful

3. We saw a cartoon about _____ mice who live in Alaska.

  a. five young funny   b. five funny young

4. We bought _____ sleeping bags for our camping trip.

  a. three warm blue   b. blue three warm

5. Dad took pictures of _____ grizzly bears.

  a. two enormous brown   b. two brown enormous

6. The painting depicts _____ fishing boats.

  a. three yellow wooden small   b. three small yellow wooden

Order Adjectives

Follow this order when using more than one adjective to describe a noun: number (**four, many, several**), opinion (**honest, friendly**), size (**smaller, tiny**), look/feel (**sticky, lumpy**), age (**recent, newborn**), shape (**round, square**), color (**pastel, translucent**), origin (**Chinese, Kenyan**), material (**paper, wooden**). There should be a comma after each adjective except after an adjective that is a number. A comma is never used between the last adjective and the noun.

Incorrect: Jake the Clown wore three, woolen, lumpy, old, caps.

Correct: Jake the Clown wore **three lumpy, old, woolen** caps.

Write the given adjectives on the line to complete each sentence. Make sure to order the adjectives correctly and use commas correctly.

1. I need the _____ boxes that you have.

    square   blue   cardboard   biggest

2. Chester is Aunt Suzy's _____ sheepdog.

    tan   mature   friendly

3. I placed _____ stones in my aquarium.

    round   several   small

4. The filmmaker got footage of a _____ apes.

    large   dozen   brown

5. The moon looked like a _____ plate against the dark sky.

    silver   round   dazzling

6. The _____ colts stood up in the stall.

    newborn   wobbly   two

Interrogative Pronouns

An interrogative pronoun is used to introduce a question. The pronouns **who**, **whom**, **what**, **which**, and **whose** are interrogative pronouns. Use **who** and **whom** for questions about people. Use **what** for questions about animals or things. Use **which** for people, animals, or things. Use **whose** to ask questions having to do with the possession of something.

Who is your teacher?

To **whom** will you give the ticket?

What is the weather forecast?

Which flavor would you like?

Whose bike is that?

Write the correct interrogative pronoun to complete each sentence.

1. _____ wants to go hiking with me next week?

2. _____ umbrella is this?

3. _____ Olympic athlete has won the most gold medals?

4. _____ cake would you rather have—the chocolate or the strawberry?

5. _____ holiday is celebrated in July?

6. _____ wants to help me plant flowers in the garden?

7. _____ was the final score of the game?

8. _____ scored the most runs?

Interrogative Pronouns

The pronouns **who**, **whom**, **what**, **which**, and **whose** are interrogative pronouns. These pronouns are used to introduce a question. Use **who** and **whom** for questions about people. Use **what** for questions about animals and things. Use **which** for people, animals, or things. Use **whose** to ask questions having to do with the possession of something. Be careful not to confuse the interrogative pronoun **whose** with the contraction **who's**.

Circle the pronoun error in each sentence. Then rewrite the sentence using the correct interrogative pronoun.

1. What of these recipes will we use to make the soup?

_____

2. What wants to play basketball this afternoon?

_____

3. Who library book is this?

_____

4. Whom way are you heading?

_____

5. Who's parents plan to attend the picnic?

_____

6. Which did you score in the last game?

_____

Complete Sentences

A complete sentence contains a subject and a verb, and expresses a complete thought. A fragment is missing a subject or a verb or both and does not express a complete thought.

Fragment Missing a Verb: Otters most of their life in water.

Complete Sentence: Otters **spend** most of their life in water.

Fragment Missing a Subject: Propel them through water.

Complete Sentence: Their flattened tails propel them through water.

Circle the phrase in ( ) that tells what the fragment is missing. Rewrite the fragment correctly as a sentence using one of the phrases below.

1. Keeps its body from drying out. (missing a subject, missing a verb)
A reptile's skin   Is useful

_____

2. In the cold, reptiles. (missing a subject, missing a verb)
slow-moving   become sluggish

_____

3. Some reptiles in very cold temperatures. (missing a subject, missing a verb)
hibernate   or snakes

_____

4. Are found in many habitats. (missing a subject, missing a verb)
May exist   Reptile homes

_____

5. The heaviest reptiles saltwater crocodiles. (missing a subject, missing a verb)
are   and alligators

_____

Precise Language

Precise written language gives the reader a better visual of the places, events, or anything else that is described.

General	Precise
ate	devoured, picked at
fruit	strawberry, pear, pomegranate
building	Empire State Building, Capitol Building
said	bellowed, cried, demanded
walked	stomped, strolled, waddled

General: I walked to the elevator.

Precise: I **strolled** to the elevator.

General: I ate the fruit.

Precise: I **devoured** the **strawberries.**

For each sentence, circle the word that is more precise. Write the word on the line to complete the sentence.

1. The tall _____ stood alone at the top of the hill.

    tree   oak

2. Jose _____ to the finish line.

    sprinted   ran

3. The bluebird _____ outside my window.

    sang   warbled

4. I was able to _____ this desk with help from Dad.

    make   construct

5. The sudden _____ took us all by surprise.

    downpour   rain

6. There was a _____ roar from the crowd when our team won.

    loud   deafening

Compound Sentences with Coordinating Conjunctions

A compound sentence is formed by using a comma and a coordinating conjunction to join two or more complete thoughts. The words **and**, **or**, **but**, **for**, **nor**, **so**, and **yet** are coordinating conjunctions.

I went into the store. My sister waited outside.

I went into the store, **but** my sister waited outside.

Write the coordinating conjunction that best completes each compound sentence. Choose one of the following: *and, or, but, for, nor, so, yet.*

1. I saw the movie, _____ I thought the book was much better.

2. Lightning flashed across the sky, _____ thunder soon followed.

3. Would you like to sell tickets, _____ do you want to help

with refreshments?

4. Paul did not enjoy rowing, _____ did he care for hiking.

5. I wanted to go to the gym, _____ it was sure to close before I

could get there.

6. It was a sunny day, _____ we used plenty of sunscreen.

7. Matt did not try out for the basketball team, _____ did he try out

for the baseball team.

Modal Auxiliaries

A modal auxiliary is a verb that helps add meaning to the main verb. The words **can**, **may**, **might**, **must**, **should**, and **would** are modal auxiliaries. **Can** expresses an ability to do something. **May** and **might** express permission or a probability. **Must** expresses a necessity. **Should** expresses something that is expected. **Would** expresses a desire or willingness to do something.

Circle the modal auxiliary that best completes the sentence. Then write the word on the line.

1. It's cloudy, so I _____ take an umbrella.

    should   can

2. You _____ see the principal now.

    would   may

3. I _____ easily find someone to help us with the fund-raiser.

    can   would

4. If it keeps snowing, we _____ have a snow day tomorrow.

    might   can

5. We _____ buy our tickets early, or they'll sell out.

    may   must

6. I _____ like to order a fruit smoothie, please.

    may   would

7. I told Carrie that I _____ be able to meet her at the store.

    would   might

Name _____ Date _____

Frequently Confused Words

Homophones are words that sound the same but have different spellings and different meanings. Some homophones are **break/brake, principal/principle, passed/past, lead/led**. Homophones can frequently be confused in writing. Make sure to think about the meaning of a homophone and use the word with the meaning intended in the sentence.

I didn't see you sitting **there**.

They're going to the movies now.

Is that **their** dog?

Circle the homophone in ( ) that correctly completes each sentence. Then place a check mark next to the correct definition of the word.

1. Cell phones are not (allowed, aloud) in many classrooms.

_____ able to be heard   _____ permitted

2. Some of the old water pipes were made of (led, lead) rather than copper.

_____ a type of metal   _____ showed the way

3. The thunderstorm (past, passed) through town quickly.

_____ from a former time or place   _____ went by

4. Let's watch (their, there) soccer team practice.

_____ a possessive pronoun   _____ a place

5. Doug spent a (weak, week) working on his science project.

_____ not strong   _____ seven days

6. We nailed a heavy (board, bored) over the broken window.

_____ a piece of wood   _____ not interested

7. (Whose, Who's) ready to leave for the game?

_____ interrogative pronoun   _____ contraction of **who is**

Grammar, Spelling & Vocabulary Activity Book • © Benchmark Education Company, LLC   G4 U10 W1 BLM1

Order Adjectives

Follow this order when using more than one adjective to describe a noun: number (**many, several, twenty**), opinion (**exciting, smart**), size (**little, tall**), look/feel (**chilly, cuddly**), age (**twelve-year-old, young**), shape (**round, square**), color (**pinkish, colorful**), origin (**lunar, southern**), material (**paper, wooden**). Use a comma after each adjective except after an adjective that is a number. Never use a comma between the last adjective and the noun.

Incorrect: The five, wooden, little, trains went round and round the narrow track.

Correct: The **five little, wooden** trains went round and round the narrow track.

Circle the letter showing the correct order of the adjectives that describe the underlined noun. Then write the adjectives on the line using correct punctuation.

1. Maura has collected _____ <u>seashells</u> over the years.

    a. large colorful many   b. many large colorful

2. Brutus, a _____ <u>German shepherd</u>, won the dog show.

    a. smart young   b. young smart

3. When he dropped his ice cream, my _____ <u>brother</u> began to cry.

    a. disappointed four-year-old   b. four-year-old disappointed

4. On the floor of the main hall were _____ <u>rugs</u>.

    a. round two beautiful large   b. two beautiful large round

Interrogative Pronouns and Relative Pronouns

An interrogative pronoun introduces a question. A relative pronoun introduces a clause that tells more information about the subject of a sentence. Some examples of interrogative and relative pronouns include **who**, **whom**, **whose**, **that**, and **which**. The way the pronoun is used in a sentence determines whether it is an interrogative or a relative pronoun.

>**Interrogative Pronouns: What** are your plans today?
>**Which** movie would you like to see?
>**Who** else would like to come? **Whose** mom is taking us?
>
>**Relative Pronouns:** My friend **who** lives down the block is coming, too. We can take the sandwiches **that** you made. The latest animated movie, **which** my brother has seen, is very good.

Circle the correct interrogative pronoun or relative pronoun in ( ) to complete each sentence.

1. (Who, What) wants to see the movie (what, that) Jan recommended?

2. (Which, Who) dog is the one (which, that) saved the boy's life?

3. (Who, Whose) wants to picnic in Oak Park, (which, what) happens to be my favorite park?

4. (Whose, Who) neighborhood is the one (whose, that) was hit by the tornado?

5. (What, Which) friend is the one (that, who) walks to school with you?

6. (Who, What) would like the extra ticket (whose, that) I bought?

Grammar, Spelling & Vocabulary Activity Book • © Benchmark Education Company, LLC   G4 U10 W2 BLM1

Correct Run-Ons

A run-on sentence contains two or more complete sentences that should be written separately or combined using a comma and a coordinating conjunction such as **and, but, or, so, for, nor,** or **yet**.

> **Run-On:** I walked to the store I bought eggs and milk.
> **Corrected:** I walked to the store, **and** I bought eggs and milk.

Circle the coordinating conjunction in ( ) that best joins the two clauses of the run-on sentence. Rewrite the run-on sentence as a compound sentence using the coordinating conjunction and correct punctuation.

1. Mia used to live near me she recently moved to Florida. (but, or)

_____

2. Adina took voice lessons soon she began winning talent shows. (but, and)

_____

3. I couldn't make it to the market yesterday I had to go today. (for, so)

_____

4. Jesse didn't want to take drum lessons he did want to take piano lessons. (nor, but)

_____

5. I'm allergic to almost all animals I'd like to get a job walking dogs. (and, yet)

_____

6. You can sell tickets you can help people find their seats. (but, or)

_____

Prepositional Phrases

A prepositional phrase includes a preposition and its object along with any modifiers. Prepositional phrases often answer one of the following questions: **which one? where? when? how? how long?**

Which one?	The boy **in** the blue sweater is my brother.
Where?	The red pencil is **in** the desk drawer.
When?	I will see you **after** recess.
How?	She went into the dark cave **with** all her courage.
How long?	The man was lost in the woods **for** two days.

In each sentence, write the preposition that best begins the prepositional phrase and answers the question in ( ).

1. _____ breakfast, we washed the dishes.
   (When?)

2. The book _____ the shiny cover was written by my friend.
   (Which one?)

3. It has been snowing _____ several hours.
   (How long?)

4. Mark accidentally knocked over the mug _____ his backpack.
   (How?)

5. I always fold my T-shirts and put them _____ my drawer.
   (Where?)

6. The girl _____ the red dress is a talented musician.
   (Which one?)

Name _____ Date _____

Prepositional Phrases

A prepositional phrase is a group of words that includes a preposition with a noun or pronoun along with any modifiers. There are many prepositions in English, such as **with, for, to, between, except, toward,** and **after.** When the object of a preposition is a pronoun or pronouns, use an object pronoun. The pronouns **me, you, him, her, it, us,** and **them** are object pronouns.

Incorrect: Sean practiced soccer kicks with I.
Correct: Sean practiced soccer kicks **with me**.

Incorrect: Sean practiced soccer kicks with Crystal and I.
Correct: Sean practiced soccer kicks **with Crystal** and **me**.
Sean practiced soccer kicks **with her** and **me**.

Underline the preposition in each sentence. Then circle the correct pronoun or pronouns in ( ).

1. Julio kicked the soccer ball between Erin and (I, me).

2. Then I kicked the ball toward (he, him).

3. In the first thirty minutes, no one scored a goal except Erin,

Julio, and (I, me).

4. Did your dad wave to (you, I) and (they, them)?

5. Yes, and the crowd cheered for (we, us).

6. Erin likes playing soccer on the same team with Julio and (I, me).

7. After the game, I had pizza with (she, her).

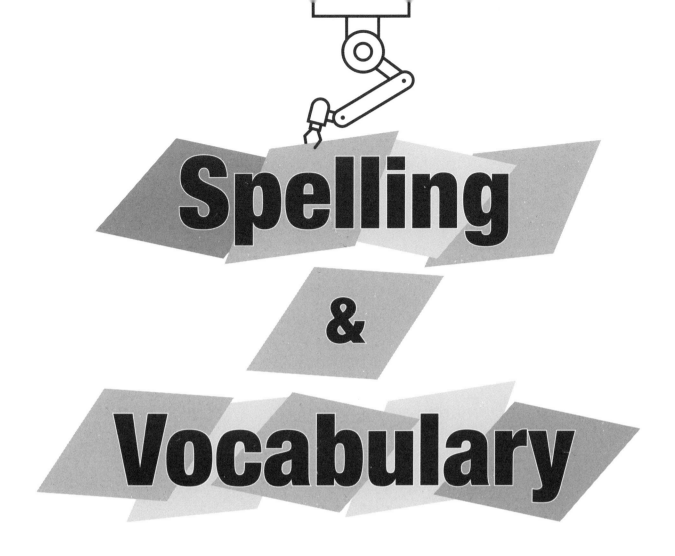

Spelling & Vocabulary

Long a and Short a

greatly	maintain	natural	staff
locate	national	spray	trails

Write a spelling word to complete each sentence.

1. Each year we help pick up litter on the hiking _____.

2. I could not _____ the hotel on the map.

3. The bank robbery made the _____ news.

4. Earth's _____ resources should be protected.

5. The bike's cost _____ exceeded my savings.

6. We try to _____ a balance between work and fun.

7. The elephants began to _____ water on each other.

8. How many teachers are on the _____ of Riverview Elementary?

Write the spelling word that is a synonym or an antonym of the bold word.

9. find synonym: _____

10. artificial antonym: _____

Name _____ Date _____

Long a and Short a

greatly	maintain	natural	staff
locate	national	spray	trails

Write the spelling words for the given number of syllables.

Spelling words with 1 syllable

1. _____   **2.** _____

3. _____

Spelling words with 2 syllables

4. _____   **5.** _____

6. _____

Spelling words with 3 syllables

7. _____   **8.** _____

Write the spelling word for each definition.

9. to find _____

10. real; not fake _____

11. crew; personnel _____

12. fine mist _____

Name _____ Date _____

Long e and Short e

centuries	everyone	overseas	residents
easy	geography	representative	these

Write the spelling word that goes with the other words.

1. all, each person, _____

2. dwellers, neighbors, _____

3. abroad, foreign, _____

4. era, 100 years, _____

5. study of land, maps, _____

6. that, those, _____

7. effortless, simple, _____

8. agent, delegate, _____

Fill in the boxes for the spelling word *easy*.

meaning	sentence
example	**related words** Synonym: Antonym: Adverb: Comparative: Superlative:

Long e and Short e

centuries	everyone	overseas	residents
easy	geography	representative	these

Write the spelling words for the given number of syllables.

Spelling word with 1 syllable

1. _____

Spelling word with 2 syllables

2. _____

Spelling words with 3 syllables

3. _____ 4. _____ 5. _____

6. _____

Spelling word with 4 syllables

7. _____

Spelling word with 5 syllables

8. _____

For each bold word, write the spelling word or words that rhyme with it.

9. freeze _____ _____ _____

10. breezy _____

Long o and Short o

bowl	floating	goes	most
dome	from	governor	shopping

Write a spelling word to complete each sentence.

1. The tournament took place in the new soccer _____.

2. Mr. Allora was the _____ interesting speaker we've ever had.

3. The campers had fun _____ down the river in the kayak.

4. Mom took me _____ for new shoes.

5. Our neighbors moved here _____ Seattle.

6. The marching band usually _____ out for pizza after practice.

Write the spelling word that completes each analogy.

7. Fork is to **plate** as **spoon** is to _____.

8. Come is to **go** as **to** is to _____.

9. Mayor is to **city** as _____ is to **state.**

10. Less is to **more** as **least** is to _____.

Name _____ Date _____

Long o and Short o

bowl	floating	goes	most
dome	from	governor	shopping

Write the spelling word for the given sound-spelling pattern.

Spelling words with long *o* spelled *o*

Spelling word with long *o* spelled *ow*

Spelling words with long *o* spelled *oa* or *oe*

Write a spelling word for each clue.

6. has 3 syllables _____

7. rhymes with **come** _____

8. has a double consonant and the suffix **-ing** _____

9. rhymes with **home** _____

Name _____ Date _____

Long i and Short i

admitted	ordinary	lying	sixty-six
crocodile	gigantic	right	terrified

Write a spelling word for each clue.

1. the opposite of telling the truth _____

2. very afraid _____

3. nothing special _____

4. the opposite of tiny _____

5. a large, tropical reptile _____

6. the number after sixty-five _____

7. correct _____

8. told the truth _____

Write a spelling word to complete each sentence.

9. The _____ building blocked the view.

10. Ella is _____ of spiders.

Long i and Short i

admitted	ordinary	lying	sixty-six
crocodile	gigantic	right	terrified

Write the spelling words for the given number of syllables.

Spelling word with 1 syllable   **Spelling word with 2 syllables**

1. _____   **2.** _____

Spelling words with 3 syllables

3. _____   **4.** _____

5. _____   **6.** _____

7. _____

Spelling word with 4 syllables

8. _____

Write a spelling word for each clue.

9. has a long **i** spelled **y** _____

10. has a long **i** followed by a consonant and silent **e** _____

Long u and Short u

abundant	communicate	refused	used
adult	continued	uncover	usually

Write a spelling word that is related to the other words.

1. rejected, declined, _____

2. talk, correspond, _____

3. often, frequently, _____

4. grown-up, mature, _____

5. plenty, more than enough, _____

6. reveal, make known, _____

7. kept going, didn't stop, _____

8. in the habit of, accustomed to, _____

Write the spelling word that completes each analogy.

9. Puppy is to **dog** as **child** is to _____.

10. Broom is to **sweep** as **phone** is to _____ .

11. Not enough is to **scarce** as **plenty** is to _____.

Name _____ Date _____

Long u and Short u

abundant	communicate	refused	used
adult	continued	uncover	usually

Write the spelling words for the given number of syllables.

Spelling word with 1 syllable

1. _____

Spelling words with 2 syllables

2. _____

3. _____

Spelling words with 3 syllables

4. _____

5. _____

6. _____

Spelling words with 4 syllables

7. _____

8. _____

Write the spelling word that matches the antonym or synonym.

9. antonym: **allowed** _____

10. synonym: **plentiful** _____

11. synonym: **share information** _____

12. antonym: **rarely** _____

Closed Syllables

chicken	fantasy	invented	princess
enchanted	fifteen	mixture	spunky

Write the spelling word that completes each sentence.

1. Do you know who _____ the steam engine?

2. The movie was an odd _____ of both comedy
and tragedy.

3. I needed a dozen muffins, but I made _____ just to
have extras.

4. I read a funny story about a _____ that lays purple eggs.

5. Mom has always been _____ with Ireland.

Write a spelling word for each clue.

6. queen, duchess, _____

7. drama, realistic fiction, _____

8. bold, courageous, _____

Grammar, Spelling & Vocabulary Activity Book • © Benchmark Education Company, LLC

Closed Syllables

chicken	fantasy	invented	princess
enchanted	fifteen	mixture	spunky

Write the spelling words that match each pattern.

Short *a* sound in the first syllable

1. _____

Short *e* sound in the first syllable

2. _____

Short *i* sound in the first syllable

3. _____ 4. _____ 5. _____

6. _____ 7. _____

Short *u* sound in the first syllable

8. _____

Write the spelling words that answer the questions.

9. Which spelling words have three syllables?

_____ _____ _____

10. Which spelling words have a final syllable with a long **e** sound spelled **y**?

_____ _____

Name _____ Date _____

Open Syllables

brazenly	deter	location	noticed
decided	local	nature	prevent

Write a spelling word that goes with the other words.

1. stop, keep from happening,

_____

2. made a choice, made a judgment,

_____

3. harshly, not embarrassed,

_____

4. nearby, not far,

_____

5. observed, seen,

_____

6. outdoors, animals,

_____

7. a specific place, an address,

_____

8. discourage, prevent from acting,

_____

Fill in the boxes for the spelling word *nature*.

meaning	sentence
example	**related words**
	Adjective:
	Adverb:
	Synonyms:

nature

Grammar, Spelling & Vocabulary Activity Book • © Benchmark Education Company, LLC G4 U3 W1 BLM1

Open Syllables

brazenly	deter	location	noticed
decided	local	nature	prevent

Write the spelling words for the given number of syllables.

Spelling words with 2 syllables

1. _____

2. _____

3. _____

4. _____

5. _____

Spelling words with 3 syllables

6. _____

7. _____

8. _____

Write a spelling word for each clue.

9. has the suffix **-ly**

_____

10. has the suffix **-ion**

_____

Vowel Team Syllables

because	cloudy	eagerly	people
believed	creature	groundhog	proclaimed

Write a spelling word to complete each sentence.

1. Another name for a woodchuck is a _____.

2. We hoped for a sunny day at the beach, but by noon it became _____.

3. One unusual _____ found in the ocean is the clownfish.

4. We _____ in the mayor's idea for improving the town's traffic problem.

5. We hope that more _____ will vote in this year's election.

6. Let's set the table _____ Mom needs our help.

7. The king loudly _____ that the prisoners should be released.

8. We _____ awaited the judge's decision.

Vowel Team Syllables

because	cloudy	eagerly	people
believed	creature	groundhog	proclaimed

Write the spelling words for the given vowel team syllable.

Spelling word with *au*

1. _____

Spelling words with *ea*

2. _____   3. _____

Spelling word with *ie*   **Spelling word with *eo***

4. _____   5. _____

Spelling words with *ou*

6. _____   7. _____

Spelling word with *ai*

8. _____

Write the spelling word or words that answer each question.

9. Which spelling word has three syllables? _____

10. Which spelling words have a syllable that rhymes with **tree**?

_____ _____ _____ _____

Vowel-r Syllables

birches	coverings	important	sturdy
charcoal	forests	Northeast	waterproof

Write a spelling word to complete each sentence.

1. When Mom goes scuba diving, she wears her _____ watch.

2. Manolo feels it is _____ to learn different languages.

3. Maine is in the American _____.

4. Grandpa used _____ to start a fire in the grill.

5. I picked out new window _____ for my bedroom.

Write the spelling word that goes with the other words.

6. stable, solid, _____

7. oaks, maples, _____

8. woodlands, groves, _____

Vowel-r Syllables

birches	coverings	important	sturdy
charcoal	forests	Northeast	waterproof

Write the spelling words for the given vowel-r syllable.

Spelling word with *ar*

1. _____

Spelling words with *or*

2. _____   3. _____

4. _____

Spelling words with *er*

5. _____   6. _____

Spelling word with *ir*   ### Spelling word with *ur*

7. _____   8. _____

Write the spelling word that answers each question.

9. Which spelling word is a synonym for **significant**? _____

10. Which spelling words have three syllables?

_____   _____   _____

Name _____ Date _____

Compound Words

first-rate	hot dogs	narrow-minded	three-quarters
high school	mind-boggling	post office	worn-out

Write a spelling word for each clue.

1. food for sale at a ball park _____

2. a place for mailing letters _____

3. more than a half _____

4. students are found here _____

5. unbelievable _____

6. very tired _____

7. the best quality _____

8. refuses to consider new ideas _____

 Grammar, Spelling & Vocabulary Activity Book • © Benchmark Education Company, LLC

Name _____ Date _____

Compound Words

first-rate	hot dogs	narrow-minded	three-quarters
high school	mind-boggling	post office	worn-out

Write the spelling words for the given number of syllables.

Spelling words with 2 syllables

1. _____

2. _____

3. _____

4. _____

Spelling words with 3 syllables

5. _____

6. _____

7. _____

Spelling words with 4 syllables

8. _____

Write the spelling word that is an antonym or a synonym of the bold word.

9. **energetic:** antonym _____

10. **startling:** synonym _____

11. **excellent:** synonym _____

12. **broad-minded:** antonym _____

Vowel-Consonant-e Syllables

| arrived | named | disease | raced |
| bravely | despite | navigate | safely |

Write a spelling word to complete each sentence.

1. Mia was nervous, but she _____ stepped up and gave her speech.

2. We planned the outdoor picnic _____ the threat of rain.

3. I think we will need a good map to _____ this city.

4. It was exciting to see the horses as they _____ toward the finish line.

5. The cooking instructor showed us how to _____ chop vegetables.

6. The kitten was found in the evening, so my friend _____ her Sunset.

7. My grandparents _____ at the airport an hour late.

8. Washing your hands helps avoid germs and prevent _____.

Vowel-Consonant-e Syllables

arrived	named	disease	raced
bravely	despite	navigate	safely

Write the spelling words for the given number of syllables.

Spelling words with 1 syllable

1. _____   2. _____

Spelling words with 2 syllables

3. _____   4. _____

5. _____   6. _____

7. _____

Spelling word with 3 syllables

8. _____

Write the spelling words that answer the questions.

9. Which spelling word has a first syllable that rhymes

with **save**? _____

10. Which spelling word rhymes with **placed**? _____

Name _____ Date _____

Consonant-le Syllables

| gobble | remarkable | single | struggled |
| purple | simple | startle | wiggled |

Write a spelling word to complete each sentence.

1. The evening sun made the mountains appear gold and _____.

2. The little caterpillar _____ its way across the leaf.

3. Not a _____ cupcake was left after the successful bake sale.

4. It was fun to hear the turkeys _____ as they began to eat.

5. I laughed as my brother _____ to free himself from the sleeping bag.

Write a spelling word that is related to the other two words.

6. easy, uncomplicated, _____

7. impressive, incredible, _____

8. stun, shock, _____

 Grammar, Spelling & Vocabulary Activity Book • © Benchmark Education Company, LLC   G4 U4 W3 BLM1

Name _____ Date _____

Consonant-le Syllables

gobble	remarkable	single	struggled
purple	simple	startle	wiggled

Write the spelling words for the given consonant-*le* syllables.

Spelling word with *-ble*

1. _____

Spelling words with *-ple*

2. _____   3. _____

Spelling words with *-gle*

4. _____   5. _____

6. _____

Spelling word with *-able*

7. _____

Spelling word with *-tle*

8. _____

Write the spelling words that answer the questions.

9. Which spelling word is a synonym for **squirmed**? _____

10. Which spelling word means "had difficulty doing something"?

_____

Hard and Soft c, g

carbon	energy	gasoline	importance
electricity	gallon	generate	substance

Write a spelling word to complete each sentence.

1. The sticky _____ on the floor is hard to clean.

2. The computer program can _____ millions of questions

per hour.

3. We learned about the benefits of using solar _____ to

power towns and cities.

4. One of the elements found in all plants and animals is

_____.

Write a spelling word to complete each analogy.

5. Food is to **people** as _____ is to **automobiles**.

6. Approval is to **permission** as **significance** is to _____.

7. Inch is to **yard** as **quart** is to _____.

8. Flashlight is to **battery** as **refrigerator** is to _____.

Hard and Soft c, g

carbon	energy	gasoline	importance
electricity	gallon	generate	substance

Write the spelling words for the given sound.

Spelling word with hard *c* and soft *c*

1. _____

Spelling word with hard *c*

2. _____

Spelling words with soft *c*

3. _____

4. _____

Spelling words with hard *g*

5. _____

6. _____

Spelling words with soft *g*

7. _____

8. _____

Write the spelling words that answer the questions.

9. Which spelling word has the most syllables? _____

10. Which spelling word has a final syllable that rhymes with **plate**?

_____

r-Controlled Vowels ar, or, oar, ore

according	charted	roared	stored
before	fortunately	start	victory

Write a spelling word to complete each sentence.

1. Mom _____ our camping equipment in the garage.

2. This will be the coldest winter in decades, _____ to the forecast.

3. My bike was damaged, but _____ my dad could fix it.

4. It was a real _____ when we convinced the council to build a dog park.

5. The fans _____ their approval when the team scored.

6. The librarian _____ the number of books borrowed each week.

7. I don't understand the instructions, so I may need to _____ over.

8. Delia wanted to check her messages _____ she left the house.

r-Controlled Vowels ar, or, oar, ore

according	charted	roared	stored
before	fortunately	start	victory

Write the spelling words for the given *r*-controlled vowel.

Spelling words with *ar*

1. _____

2. _____

Spelling word with *oar*

3. _____

Spelling word with *ore*

4. _____

Spelling words with *or*

5. _____

6. _____

7. _____

8. _____

Write a spelling word for each clue.

9. an antonym for **after**

_____

10. a synonym for **begin**

_____

r-Controlled Vowels er, ir, ur

curb	meters	quarter	thirds
first	percent	surrounding	thirteen

Write a spelling word for each clue.

1. penny, nickel, dime _____

2. side of a street _____

3. the opposite of last _____

4. accept money for parking spaces _____

5. fourths, halves _____

6. one more than a dozen _____

7. one part of a hundred _____

8. nearby or enclosing _____

Complete each sentence with a spelling word.

9. The workers fixed the broken _____ of the sidewalk.

10. After sitting in the waiting room for a _____ of an hour, I finally saw the doctor.

11. Jamie, Max, and Sam split the pie into _____.

12. Gabby volunteered to present _____ because she was eager to show off her hard work.

r-Controlled Vowels er, ir, ur

curb	meters	quarter	thirds
first	percent	surrounding	thirteen

Write the spelling words for the given *r*-controlled vowel.

Spelling words with *er*

1. _____   2. _____

3. _____

Spelling words with *ir*

4. _____   5. _____

6. _____

Spelling words with *ur*

7. _____   8. _____

Write the spelling words that answer the questions.

9. Which spelling words have only one syllable?

_____ _____ _____

10. Which spelling word rhymes with **heaters**? _____

Adverb Suffixes -ly, -ily, -ways, -wise

barely	counterclockwise	peacefully	speedily
clockwise	disdainfully	sideways	wildly

Write a spelling word for each clue.

1. only just enough

_____

2. direction of hour and minute hands on a clock _____

3. in a disapproving way

_____

4. quietly, agreeably

_____

5. slanted, indirect

_____

6. opposite of clockwise

_____

7. recklessly, disorderly

_____

8. extremely fast

_____

Fill in the boxes for the spelling word *peacefully*.

meaning	sentence
example	**related words** Noun: Adjective: Synonym: Antonym:

Adverb Suffixes -ly, -ily, -ways, -wise

barely	counterclockwise	peacefully	speedily
clockwise	disdainfully	sideways	wildly

Write the spelling words for the given adverb suffix.

Spelling words that end with *-ly*

1. _____   2. _____

3. _____   4. _____

Spelling word that ends with *-ily*

5. _____

Spelling word that ends with *-ways*

6. _____

Spelling words that end with *-wise*

7. _____   8. _____

Write the spelling words that answer the questions.

9. Which spelling words have three syllables?

_____   _____

10. Which spelling words have the most syllables?

_____   _____

Name _____ Date _____

Long oo and Short oo

blew	doomed	pulling	troop
could	looked	soon	would

Write a spelling word to complete each sentence.

1. Who _____ like to help clean up the park?

2. I want to finish my homework as _____ as possible.

3. I have been helping Mrs. Janos by _____ weeds out of the garden.

4. The wind _____ down many trees in our neighborhood.

5. Kim's plan to train her cat was _____ from the beginning.

6. The divers _____ for the wreckage of the ship but found nothing.

7. The cavalry _____ marched in the parade.

8. If you need help on Saturday, I _____ babysit in the afternoon.

 Grammar, Spelling & Vocabulary Activity Book • © Benchmark Education Company, LLC

Long oo and Short oo

blew	doomed	pulling	troop
could	looked	soon	would

Write the spelling words for the given sound.

Spelling words with long *oo*

1. _____   2. _____

3. _____   4. _____

Spelling words with short *oo*

5. _____   6. _____

7. _____   8. _____

Write the spelling words that answer each question.

9. Which spelling word is an antonym for **late**?

_____

10. Which spelling word means "a failure that can't be avoided"?

_____

Adjective Suffixes
-ful, -ous, -ible, -able, -some

dangerous	fearsome	invincible	resourceful
famous	honorable	painful	troublesome

Write a spelling word for each clue.

1. causing problems _____

2. quick-thinking _____

3. very well-known _____

4. unsafe; likely to cause injury _____

5. trustworthy _____

6. impossible to defeat _____

7. frightening, terrifying _____

8. aching, hurting _____

Adjective Suffixes
-ful, -ous, -ible, -able, -some

dangerous	fearsome	invincible	resourceful
famous	honorable	painful	troublesome

Write the spelling words for the given adjective suffix.

Spelling words that end with *-ful*

1. _____   2. _____

Spelling words that end with *-ous*

3. _____   4. _____

Spelling word that ends with *-ible*

5. _____

Spelling word that ends with *-able*

6. _____

Spelling words that end with *-some*

7. _____   8. _____

Complete each sentence with a spelling word.

9. When faced with a problem, Mia is _____ in her search

for a solution.

10. The football team has won every game this season—it appears to be

_____.

/ou/ and /oi/

account	brown	destroyed	pounded
boiling	county	outside	soil

Write the spelling word that best completes each sentence.

1. The carpenter _____ the nails into the

wooden boards.

2. We planted the seeds in the garden's rich _____.

3. I put some money into my savings _____

each month.

4. In which _____ does your cousin live?

5. Our new puppy _____ one of Mom's shoes.

6. Once the water began _____, we put the pasta

into the pot.

Write the spelling word that best completes each analogy.

7. Gray is to **black** as **beige** is to _____.

8. Cold is to **hot** as **freezing** is to _____.

9. Down is to **up** as _____ is to **inside**.

10. Built is to **created** as **demolished** is to _____.

/ou/ and /oi/

account	brown	destroyed	pounded
boiling	county	outside	soil

Write the spelling words for the given sound-spelling pattern.

Spelling words with /ou/ spelled ou

1. _____   2. _____

3. _____   4. _____

Spelling word with /ou/ spelled ow

5. _____

Spelling words with /oi/ spelled oi

6. _____   7. _____

Spelling word with /oi/ spelled oy

8. _____

Write the spelling word that matches each definition.

9. an area that is part of a state   10. hit with force again and

again

_____   _____

11. dirt where plants grow

_____

Name _____ Date _____

Prefixes trans-, pro-, sub-, super-, inter-

interfered	proceeded	substituted	transcontinental
intervals	progress	superstars	transport

Write a spelling word for each clue.

1. took the place of

_____

2. across land

_____

3. meddled

_____

4. continued on

_____

5. extremely famous

_____

6. improvement

_____

7. time between events

_____

8. take from one place to another

_____

Fill in the boxes for the spelling word *progress*.

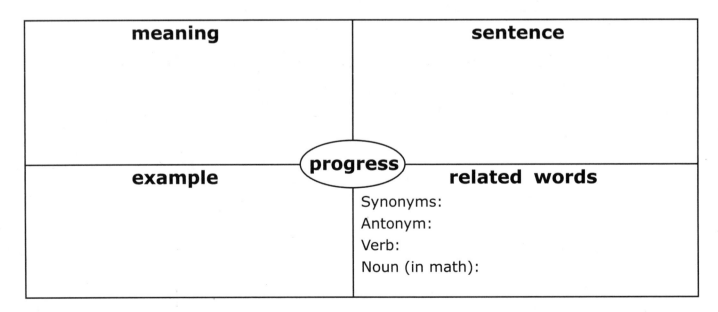

meaning	sentence
example	**related words**
	Synonyms: Antonym: Verb: Noun (in math):

progress

Grammar, Spelling & Vocabulary Activity Book • © Benchmark Education Company, LLC   G4 U7 W2 BLM1

Name _____ Date _____

Prefixes trans-, pro-, sub-, super-, inter-

interfered	proceeded	substituted	transcontinental
intervals	progress	superstars	transport

Write the spelling words for the given prefix.

Spelling words that begin with *inter-*

1. _____   2. _____

Spelling words that begin with *pro-*

3. _____   4. _____

Spelling words that begin with *sub-* or *super-*

5. _____   6. _____

Spelling words that begin with *trans-*

7. _____   8. _____

Write the spelling word that matches each clue.

9. switched one thing for another

10. people who excel at what they do

_____   _____

Homophones

blue	rained	there	wait
dear	side	to	week

In each sentence, fill in the blanks with a spelling word and its homophone. Choose one of the following homophones: *blew, deer, reigned, sighed, their, too, weight, weak*.

1. The _____ flag _____ in the wind.

2. A _____ friend of mine likes to feed _____.

3. It _____ frequently during the time the queen _____.

4. He _____ when he realized he forgot to paint one _____.

5. Students return _____ library books over _____.

6. I want _____ go to Hawaii, _____!

7. _____ until you find out the _____ of the apples.

8. Exercising three times a _____ will strengthen your _____ muscles.

Name _____ Date _____

Homophones

blue	rained	there	wait
dear	side	to	week

Write the spelling words for the given sound-spelling pattern.

Spelling words with long *e* spelled *ea* or *ee*

1. _____   2. _____

Spelling words with long *a* spelled *ai*

3. _____   4. _____

Spelling word with long *u* spelled *ue*

5. _____

Spelling word with long *i* spelled with a vowel-consonant-*e* pattern

6. _____

Write a spelling word for each clue.

7. homophone of **too** and **two**   8. homophone of **their** and **they're**

_____   _____

Negative Prefixes de-, un-, in-, im-, dis-

| destruction | impossible | insignificant | unprepared |
| disappeared | incredibly | unbelievable | unaware |

Write a spelling word for each clue.

1. vanished, no longer seen _____

2. unimaginable, unthinkable _____

3. extraordinarily _____

4. not conscious of _____

5. not ready _____

6. unimportant _____

7. cannot happen _____

8. ruination, wrecking _____

Write a spelling word to complete each sentence.

9. My notebook _____, so I cleaned my room to try and find it.

10. It would be _____ to run two marathons in one day.

Name _____ Date _____

Negative Prefixes de-, un-, in-, im-, dis-

| destruction | impossible | insignificant | unprepared |
| disappeared | incredibly | unbelievable | unaware |

Write the spelling words for the given negative prefixes.

Spelling words that begin with *un-*

1. _____ 2. _____

3. _____

Spelling words that begin with *in-*

4. _____ 5. _____

Spelling word that begins with *de-*

6. _____

Spelling word that begins with *dis-*

7. _____

Spelling word that begins with *im-*

8. _____

Write the spelling word that is formed from the root word in bold.

9. believe _____

10. prepare _____

Greek and Latin Roots geo, archae, rupt

archaeologists	erupt	eruption	geologists
disrupted	erupted	geological	geology

Write the spelling word that completes each sentence.

1. The volcanic _____ caused widespread damage.

2. Many _____ study the layers of rock in the Grand Canyon.

3. This book about _____ has lots of pictures of fossils.

4. The _____ dug up the site to find the ruins and learn more about how the people of the ancient civilization lived.

5. It is difficult to predict when a volcano might _____.

6. The scientists studied the _____ deposits left by the ice sheets.

7. Our plans were _____ by the unexpected blizzard.

8. When Mount St. Helens _____ in 1980, it changed the landscape of the mountain.

Greek and Latin Roots geo, archae, rupt

| archaeologists | erupt | eruption | geologists |
| disrupted | erupted | geological | geology |

Write the spelling words for the given roots.

Spelling words with *geo*

1. _____   2. _____

3. _____

Spelling word with *archae*

4. _____

Spelling words with *rupt*

5. _____   6. _____

7. _____   8. _____

Write the spelling words that answer the questions.

9. Which spelling words have the suffix **-ist**?

_____

10. Which spelling word has the suffix **-ion**?

_____

Name _____ Date _____

Variant Vowel /ô/

August	chalky	fall	stall
causing	dawn	pause	talking

Write a spelling word for each clue.

1. another word for **speaking** _____

2. the opposite of dusk _____

3. to take a short break _____

4. making something happen _____

5. a shade of white _____

6. one of the twelve months of the year _____

7. a small holding area for an animal _____

8. tumble _____

Write a spelling word to complete each sentence.

9. We woke up before _____ to drive
to the airport.

10. I enjoy _____ to my friends
on the phone.

Variant Vowel /ô/

August	chalky	fall	stall
causing	dawn	pause	talking

Write the spelling words for the given spelling patterns.

Spelling words with *au*

1. _____   2. _____

3. _____

Spelling words with *al*

4. _____   5. _____

6. _____   7. _____

Spelling words with *aw*

8. _____

Write the spelling words that answer the questions.

9. Which spelling words have first syllables that rhyme?

_____

10. Which spelling word has a final syllable that rhymes with **must**?

_____

Noun Suffixes -dom, -ity, -tion, -ment, -ness

| community | employment | kindness | registration |
| agreements | equality | organization | wisdom |

Write a spelling word to complete each sentence.

1. The theme of the candidate's speech was _____.

2. Pam and Beth each signed legal _____ during the court case.

3. The _____ for summer softball leagues will begin at noon.

4. The parks department is looking for lifeguards for summer _____.

5. The company was bought by a large _____.

Write the spelling word that is related to the other words.

6. town, village, _____

7. good judgment, intelligence, _____

8. courtesy, goodness, _____

Noun Suffixes -dom, -ity, -tion, -ment, -ness

community	employment	kindness	registration
agreements	equality	organization	wisdom

Write the spelling words for the given noun suffix.

Spelling word with *-dom*   **Spelling word with *-ness***

1. _____   2. _____

Spelling words with *-ity*

3. _____   4. _____

Spelling words with *-tion*

5. _____   6. _____

Spelling words with *-ment*

7. _____   8. _____

Write the spelling word that is formed from the bold base word.

9. equal _____

10. wise _____

Latin Roots mis, agri, duc/duct, man

agriculture	introduced	manual	missiles
intermission	manipulate	manufactured	produced

Write a spelling word for each clue.

1. pause

_____

2. made on a large scale

_____

3. created

_____

4. weapons that are launched

_____

5. handbook

_____

6. first brought into practice or use

_____

7. to take advantage of

_____

8. the science of working the land

_____

Fill in the boxes for the spelling word *manufactured*.

meaning	sentence
example — manufactured — **related words**	
	Verb: Noun: Synonyms:

Latin Roots mis, agri, duc/duct, man

agriculture	introduced	manual	missiles
intermission	manipulate	manufactured	produced

Write the spelling words for the given Latin root.

Spelling words with *mis*

1. _____

2. _____

Spelling word with *agri*

3. _____

Spelling words with *duc*

4. _____

5. _____

Spelling words with *man*

6. _____

7. _____

8. _____

Write the spelling words that answer the following questions.

9. Which spelling words have the suffix **-ed**?

_____   _____   _____

10. Which spelling word has a final syllable that rhymes with **rate**?

_____

Variant Vowel /âr/

carefully	despair	prepare	tears
declares	forbearance	repaired	wears

Write a spelling word to complete each sentence.

1. I need to _____ notes for my speech.

2. The losing team began to _____ of ever winning again.

3. When we examined the fabric, we found a number of _____ in the cotton.

4. A governor often _____ a state of emergency after a natural disaster.

5. I made my way_____ across the icy sidewalk.

6. The pilgrims showed an incredible amount of patience and _____.

7. Too much or too little air in tires _____ down their tread faster than any other cause.

8. I made sure the brakes on my bike were _____ before the race.

Variant Vowel /âr/

carefully	despair	prepare	tears
declares	forbearance	repaired	wears

Write the spelling words for the given spelling pattern.

Spelling words with *are*

1. _____

2. _____

3. _____

Spelling words with *air*

4. _____

5. _____

Spelling words with *ear*

6. _____

7. _____

8. _____

Write the spelling words that answer the following questions.

9. Which spelling words have three syllables?

_____ _____

10. Which spelling words have a final syllable that rhymes with **chair**?

_____

Adding Endings

emergencies	humming	snagged	unluckier
grabbed	resumed	stifling	whined

Write a spelling word to complete each sentence.

1. It was a hot and humid day, and the classroom was _____.

2. Of the two hopeless contestants, it's hard to say who was

_____.

3. Millie _____ that she never got chosen first.

4. With all the air conditioners on, there was a distinct

_____ sound.

5. After a short break to stretch our legs, we _____ our

committee meeting.

6. We learned how to be prepared for all types of _____.

7. I'm glad I _____ a few pieces of fruit before heading out.

8. Jeremy got to the ticket office early and _____ tickets

for the best seats!

Name _____ Date _____

Adding Endings

emergencies	humming	snagged	unluckier
grabbed	resumed	stifling	whined

Write the spelling words for which the given ending rule applies.

Drop the final _y_.

1. _____   2. _____

Double the final consonant.

3. _____   4. _____

5. _____

Drop the final _e_.

6. _____   7. _____

8. _____

Read each word. Then write the spelling word that rhymes with it.

9. bagged

10. dined

_____   _____

Words with Final /əl/ and /ən/

barren	controversial	fossil	metropolitan
chemical	essential	kitchen	travels

Write the spelling word that best completes each sentence.

1. Rosa plans to visit every continent and write a blog about her

_____.

2. In the winter, the landscape looked like a _____ wasteland.

3. San Francisco is one of America's major _____ areas.

4. After the ship crashed, there was concern about a

_____ spill.

Write a spelling word that goes with the other words.

5. questionable, disputed, _____

6. living room, dining room, _____

7. necessary, crucial, _____

8. relic, skeleton, _____

 Grammar, Spelling & Vocabulary Activity Book • © Benchmark Education Company, LLC

Words with Final /əl/ and /ən/

barren	controversial	fossil	metropolitan
chemical	essential	kitchen	travels

Write the spelling words for the final sound-spelling pattern.

Final /əl/ sound spelled *al*

1. _____   2. _____

3. _____

Final /əl/ sound spelled *el*

4. _____

Final /əl/ sound spelled *il*

5. _____

Final /ən/ sound spelled *en*

6. _____   7. _____

Final /ən/ sound spelled *an*

8. _____

Write a spelling word to answer each question.

9. Which word has a first syllable that rhymes with **jet**? _____

10. Which word has a first syllable that rhymes with **rich**? _____

Latin and Greek Roots

audibly	autograph	inventor	transmitting
audience	emigrated	shadowgraphs	venue

Write the spelling word that matches each clue.

1. place where an event is held _____

2. someone's signature _____

3. group gathered to hear or see something _____

4. sending from one place to another _____

5. way of speaking that allows you to be heard _____

6. person who creates the first one of something _____

7. left a country or region to live elsewhere _____

8. what early x-ray images were called _____

Latin and Greek Roots

audibly	autograph	inventor	transmitting
audience	emigrated	shadowgraphs	venue

Write the spelling words for the given Latin or Greek root.

Spelling words with *ven*

1. _____   2. _____

Spelling word with *migr*

3. _____

Spelling words with *graph*

4. _____   5. _____

Spelling word with *mit*

6. _____

Spelling words with *aud*

7. _____   8. _____

Write a spelling word to answer each question.

9. Which word is related to the word **migrate**? _____

10. Which word has a double consonant and an **-ing** ending?

_____